SETTLING
· IN ·
MICHIGAN
And other true pioneer stories

Retold by
Lynne Deur

Illustrated by
Don Ellens

River Road Publications, Inc.

Author's Note

Some of our richest history comes from the informal stories of the people who lived it. In this collection I have attempted to make some of these texts accessible to young people. Although in many instances this process required editing and adapting, I tried to keep the changes at a minimum so that the voices you hear are indeed those of Michigan's pioneers.

ISBN: 0-938682-22-9

Published by River Road Publications, Inc., Spring Lake, Michigan 49456

Contents

A Pioneer Song

In the 1830s this song was popular in Michigan. Here are some of the sixteen verses that were once sung by Perrin Moe of Jackson County.

Come, all you Yankee farmers who would like to change your lot,
Who have spunk enough to travel beyond your native
    spot,
And leave behind the country where pa and ma doth
    stay,
Then come and make your fortune in Michigania.

'Tis you that talk of Vermont; why, what a place is
that?
Be sure the girls are pretty and the cattle very fat;
But who would like on mountains the clouds and snow
to stay,
When you can buy prairies in Michigania?

This land is quite productive and everything for use,
A plenty of good cider and also maple juice;
The grape, the plum, the cherry, and apples grow this
    way,
And quite delicious peaches in Michigania.

The rivers, creeks and lakes abound with excellent fish,
And in the woods wild turkeys, which make a dainty
    dish;
The bear, the elk, the buffalo, buck, doe and fawn doth
    stray,
And many other kinds of game in Michigania.

Come, all you Yankee farmers, who have muckle
hearts like me,
And elbow grease in plenty, to bow the forest tree;
Come, take a quarter section, and I'll be bound to say,
You never'll regret your coming to Michigania.

West - In the first part of the 1800s, the West generally meant the Northwest Territory. It included states we now know as Ohio, Indiana, Michigan, Illinois, and Wisconsin, along with northeastern Minnesota.

N.E
Minnesota
Statehood
1858

U.P.

Wisconsin
Statehood
1848

Michigan
Statehood
1837

Illinois
Statehood
1818

Indiana
Statehood
1816

Ohio
Statehood
1803

Introduction

Don't go to Michigan, that land of ills;
The word means ague, fever, and chills.

Over 150 years ago that little rhyme was popular in the eastern part of the United States. It was meant to be a warning, with a little humor, to all the people who were rushing to settle in the **West**. Fur traders, soldiers, and settlers who had already gone to the Michigan Territory complained of getting ague (A gyoo). That was a sickness with fever and chills which seemed to return again and again. Most people believed that Michigan's many swamps somehow caused ague. That was partly right. The sickness came from mosquitoes that lived in the swamps.

Of course, pioneers did finally come to Michigan. But many preferred to settle in Ohio, Indiana, and Illinois. These areas had thousands of acres of great farmland, while Michigan had

thousands of acres of forest that had to be cleared to make farmland. The other states were on the main trails west. Michigan was out of the way. A large swamp blocked settlers who tried to travel through the northwestern corner of Ohio and into Michigan Territory.

A new and better route was opened to the Michigan Territory in 1825. This was the Erie Canal which crossed New York State from Albany to Buffalo. Once people traveled to Buffalo by canal boat, they could take a large sailboat or a steamboat across Lake Erie to Detroit.

But getting to Michigan was just the first adventure for settlers. There were only a few rugged roads or trails branching out from Detroit. People had to walk or take wagons through thick forests and large swamps to find land where they could begin farming.

Once settlers bought land, they had to cut down giant trees. They built log cabins and plowed the land around tree stumps so they could plant crops. If they had farm animals, they had to protect them from wild animals and keep them from getting lost in the forest. A pioneer family simply had to work hard every day to make a life in the wilderness.

Who were these people who came to the Michigan Territory in the early 1800s? Most of them came from New York and from New England states such as Massachusetts and New Hampshire. Some settlers moved to Michigan from Ohio and Indiana. A few came from Virginia and North Carolina. Some pioneers came from other countries, such as Canada, Ireland, and Germany.

We are lucky that a few of these pioneers wrote about their experiences in Michigan. Through their writing we can better understand what life was really like at that time. But we can also see that these people were not so different from us today. They liked to laugh and have fun. They sometimes found themselves in trouble with their teacher or parents. Sometimes, too, their stories are filled with sadness.

The stories from these Michigan pioneers remind us that history is not just about important people like presidents and big events like wars. History involves people much like you and me. Events that seem to be unimportant at the time become more important as we look back and see how they shaped our lives.

The people in this book wrote their stories many years after they had lived them. They probably did this later because their lives were more settled and comfortable then. But they probably also looked back and understood that they had played a part in shaping the wilderness of the Michigan Territory into a state with rich farms and busy towns. Their stories are worth listening to as we continue to live and shape the history of Michigan.

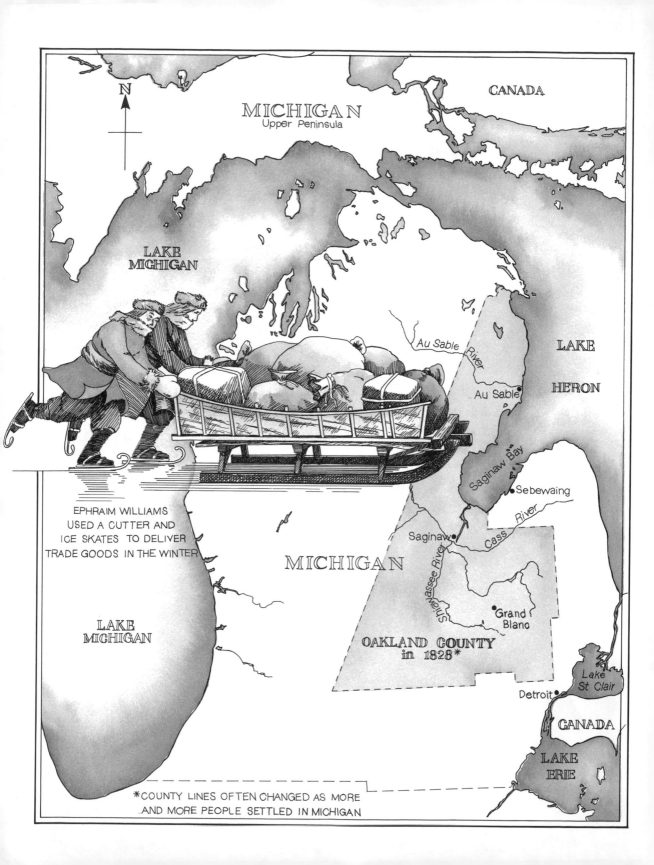

N

CANADA

MICHIGAN
Upper Peninsula

LAKE
MICHIGAN

LAKE
HERON

Au Sable River

Au Sable

Saginaw Bay

Sebewaing

Cass River

EPHRAIM WILLIAMS
USED A CUTTER AND
ICE SKATES TO DELIVER
TRADE GOODS IN THE WINTER

MICHIGAN

Saginaw

Shiawassee River

Grand
Blanc

LAKE
MICHIGAN

OAKLAND COUNTY
in 1828 *

Lake
St Clair

Detroit

CANADA

LAKE
ERIE

*COUNTY LINES OFTEN CHANGED AS MORE
AND MORE PEOPLE SETTLED IN MICHIGAN

1
A Trader's Life

Ephraim S. Williams came with his family from Massachusetts to the Michigan Territory in 1815 when he was thirteen years old. At that time the few settlers in the territory lived mainly in the Detroit area. Ephraim's father earned a living in many ways. He ran a boarding house and a trading business and he started a farm. Ephraim worked with his father for many years. Then in 1826, he and his brother started a trading business of their own.

In 1818 Father and several others set out to find land for farming. When they returned, they told others about beautiful land in Oakland County, especially a place later called Silver Lake. People were shocked, for they thought most of Michigan's land was wilderness that was not good for farming and could not be settled.

In the winter of 1818 and 1819 Father set out for Oakland County with his horses and wagon, his tools, and three men to build a home for his family. This was the first team and wagon ever driven in this area. The trip took three days since the men had to cut down trees to make a road and find places to get the wagon across streams. When they reached Pontiac, where a few settlers already lived, they put their supplies on ponies and continued the trip to Silver Lake.

Father's house was made of logs stacked nicely one and a half stories high. It was fifty feet long and twenty feet wide and had a **shake** roof. In March, 1819, he moved us in and began to make a farm among the flies, mosquitoes, snakes, wild game, and fever and **ague**. Father used to say, when asked if we had the ague, "Yes, we had a little about thirteen months in the year." Our family suffered much from sickness and the lack of the comforts of life during these years. The Indians were kind and friendly during our sickness, bringing us wild meat and berries of the best kind.

In the summer of 1820 Father built a large barn, forty feet by forty feet. It was made of planks instead of logs, with shingles on the roof. We plowed the land where we had cut logs and began to farm. It took three or four **yoke** of good heavy oxen to plow this newly cleared land. The first season we planted about six acres in wheat.

---

shake - a thin, flat piece of wood used on the side or roof of a house
ague - a sickness with fever and chills
yoke - a pair of work animals joined together by a collar
sugar gum - a gum-like material made by pouring a layer of warm, thick maple syrup on snow

---

Before it was ripe the yellow birds began coming. We were delighted by them at first. But their numbers grew larger and they destroyed every head of grain. We never cut one stalk of wheat that season, and we thought that was a rather bad start.

Father knew other ways to keep the family from starving. He kept a few trading goods, and my brothers and I gave the Indians these goods for their furs, maple sugar, and wax, or **sugar gum**. Every spring, while I was still a boy living at home, I took a load of the furs, sugar, and wax to Detroit and exchanged them for things we did not have on the farm.

When Williams grew older and left home, he became a trader. In 1825 he married Hannah Gates, and the couple had a family of seven children. They lived in a number of places, including Saginaw and Flint.

In 1828 my brother and I started the Indian trade under the name of G. D. & E. S. Williams. Our business was part of the American Fur Company. We had to go, with others in the American Fur Company, about forty miles from Saginaw to Grand Blanc. There were no roads or houses along the way. We rode ponies with our children in front of us. We had to lead the ponies through swamps or bad places and then return to carry our wives and children on our backs. In those days we often lived where all of our children's playmates were Indian children.

We established stores at River Au Sable, one at Cass River, and one at Sebewaing. Each store had a clerk and two men. We also had several Indian women trade for us. They were good traders and collected many furs. They also could be trusted with every dollar.

My brother and I owned a small sloop called the "Savage." It traveled constantly between Saginaw and Detroit. One spring cranberries were priced very high in Detroit and Buffalo. We had many berries along the lowlands of the Shiawassee River.

We told the Indians that we would buy all the cranberries they could bring us. They went picking, and we filled all the barrels and boxes on the *Savage*. I think we had almost two thousand bushels. When we got to Detroit, we heard about a man from Buffalo buying all the cranberries he could. We sold him our whole cargo, delivering them all the way to Buffalo on the *Savage*.

One bright, cold winter morning I started out from Saginaw with a helper to go to our post at River Au Sable. We wore ice skates and pushed a cutter full of trade goods in front of us. We were going with great speed down the river when our cutter hit thin ice and dropped into an air hole. We finally got back to strong ice, but some of our goods were wet, and so were we. We made a good fire, dried ourselves, and went on, leaving some wet corn and flour at an Indian camp along the way. The next day we arrived at our post at River Au Sable.

While we were at our Au Sable post, a heavy wind broke up the ice on the bay and lake. We had to leave our cutter and make our way along the shore. We made our way homeward very slowly, with packs on our backs. When we came to the camp where we had left our corn and flour, we found Indians almost starving. They could not get out on the bay and fish through the ice. The young men came in from hunting, but they had killed nothing.

I asked an Indian woman if she still had the bag from the wet flour I had given her. She brought it forward and I told her to scrape it off and cook the flour for our supper. She was pleased to do so, and made a large kettle of flour mush. She gave it to her family and a large pan of it to us. Then she saved some for our breakfast.

When we were ready to leave, an old Indian man came to me with a dried fish he had been saving. "My son," he said, "this is a cold morning. You have a very cold trip. You have nothing to eat and you will find the Indians on your route poor and hungry. Take this fish. You will need it more than I."

I thanked him but said no and handed it back to him. He would not take it. Finally I cut the fish in halves and handed him a half. He took it, and we shook hands and left.

We traveled until afternoon when it was so cold we could not stand it. We found an Indian camp where the women and children were all out digging in the snow for acorns, which was all they had to eat. We stayed with them, and when it was nearly dark their hunters came back with a large raccoon. Everyone was joyful, and we soon had a hot supper of raccoon and our half of the fish.

It was awfully cold, even though the Indians kept a fire all night. We slept very little. In the morning, without breakfast, we started walking on the rough ice of the bay. Finally we smelled the smoke from the camp of one of our Indian traders. When we arrived, we found an old man had just brought in a dozen trout from the lake. The Indian trader welcomed us into her camp, which was clean and warm. We laid down and the daughters of the trader took off our moccasins which were frozen to our feet. The girls pounded some corn, and soon we had corn stew, a kettle of fish, and bread baked in ashes. It was a feast with plenty left for breakfast. Never could anyone have been more kindly treated or better cared for than we were.

The next morning we started for home with heavy packs on our backs. We arrived about sunset and all were glad to see us. Mrs. Williams had made a New Year's dinner, hoping I would be home. After washing and changing clothes, we sat down to a splendid table, a happy home, and a happy New Year's gathering.

Not all of Ephraim Williams' life was as exciting. There were everyday problems to put up with—such as mosquitoes!

Every spring in closing up our business and leaving for Detroit where I would sell our furs, I had a good deal of writing to do. The mosquitoes were such pests! I would set a table in the middle of the store floor, with a kettle of smoke under it, and write until almost blinded. My eyes would get so sore I could hardly see, but this was the only way we could write.

Mosquitoes were just as bad in the morning when I went to get water from the river. I shut my eyes and mouth, ran to the river, filled the pail with water, and ran back as fast as I could. By the evening, horses and cattle would come running from the woods to oak openings where we had smoky fires for them to keep the mosquitoes away. The animals were black with mosquitoes and blood.

We had to enclose our beds, windows, doors, and fireplace with net. If not, mosquitoes would come in and fill the room. I never saw anything like it. As we cleared the land, there were fewer mosquitoes and they became less troublesome.

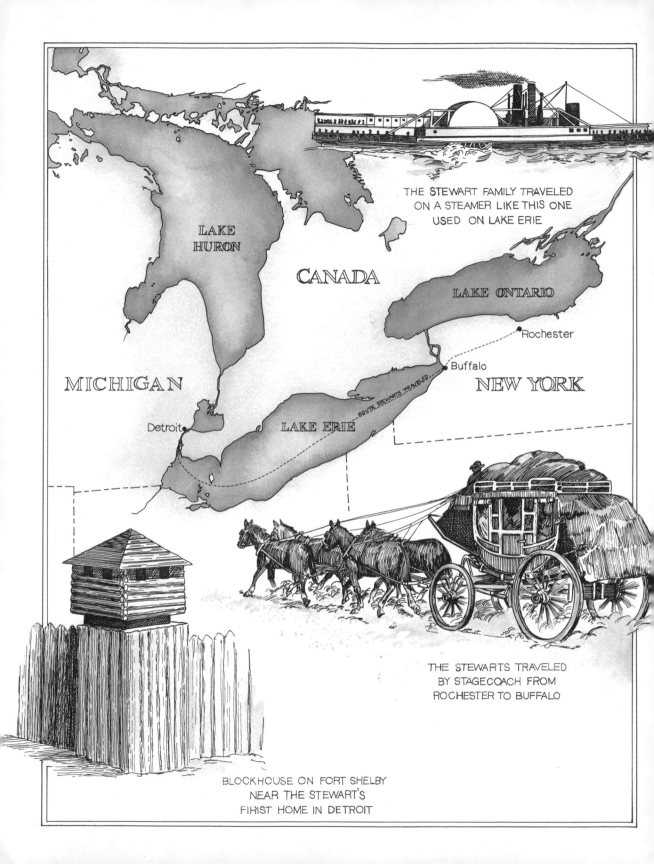

LAKE HURON

CANADA

LAKE ONTARIO

Rochester

Buffalo

MICHIGAN

NEW YORK

Detroit

ROUTE STEWARTS TRAVELED

LAKE ERIE

THE STEWART FAMILY TRAVELED ON A STEAMER LIKE THIS ONE USED ON LAKE ERIE

THE STEWARTS TRAVELED BY STAGECOACH FROM ROCHESTER TO BUFFALO

BLOCKHOUSE ON FORT SHELBY NEAR THE STEWART'S FIRST HOME IN DETROIT

2
My Childhood In Detroit

In the late 1800s, Mrs. E. M. S. Stewart wrote about her life as a child in Detroit. She traveled with her family from Rochester, New York, to Michigan Territory. Even though her family settled in Detroit instead of in a cabin in a deep forest, Mrs. Stewart remembered these pioneer days as ones of adventure and excitement.

Detroit began as a French fort in 1701. It was called Fort Pontchartrain, and it was headed by a French leader called Cadillac. Cadillac encouraged French settlers to build farms along the Detroit River.

By the time Mrs. Stewart's family came to Detroit, the Michigan area had changed from French to British to American ownership. Fort Pontchartrain, too, had changed during that time. Under the British it was called Fort Detroit. The Americans changed its name to Fort Shelby. But most of the French settlers stayed on their lands during these changes. Their children, grandchildren, and the great-grandchildren still lived on the farms along the river when Mrs. Stewart's family arrived in the early 1800s.

My father, my mother, my younger sister, and I traveled from Rochester, New York, to Detroit in 1824 when I was seven years old. We rode in a stagecoach from Rochester to Buffalo and traveled through the night so that we would not miss the steamer across Lake Erie.

I had never before seen a large body of water. I stood on the steamer's deck and watched Buffalo fade from view. As I listened to the splash, splash of the steamer's wheels in the sparkling water, my mind was filled with fear, wonder, and delight.

The three days of our trip were ones of beauty. There was not a cloud in the sky. The distant shore looked dreamy and hazy. There was not a ripple in the sleeping waters. I even wished for a storm, so I might see how white caps danced on top of the waves.

As we came up the Detroit River, the view on the American side was very cheerful. Farm houses lined the river. They were built in French style, one-story high with steep roofs. A few of them were painted white, and all of them were half hidden by tall lilac and rosebushes. A road separated the little yard in front of the house from a vegetable garden which reached to the river's edge. A wharf or dock of a single plank ran out into the river. A canoe or sailboat was tied there.

The steamer announced her approach to the city by firing a cannon. It seemed to call out the whole town. French women wearing large straw hats and carrying baskets of fruit pressed through a crowd of men and boys. Carts drawn by small ponies backed up to the edge of the wharf where we were landing, and their owners talked loudly in French and English. In the background was a coach waiting to take passengers to the only hotel in the city.

As people from "down east," we had to get used to two things in Detroit. One was the Indians who traded in the city each day. Some of them begged for food and frightened my mother, but in time she lost her fear of them. The other problem was our need for water. Our only water supply was the river. Men brought up barrels each day and sold them at high prices. Just think of drinking water without ice during the summer, after the water had stood in a wooden barrel for a day or more!

Our house was a short distance from Fort Shelby. When we first lived in Detroit, there were still some troops at the fort. Every morning and evening we could hear their bugle calls, and we often watched the soldiers parade on the fields outside the fort. In the summer of 1825 the troops were removed to Green Bay, and the fort and its grounds soon became a delightful playground for children in my neighborhood. We ran all around and peeped through the portholes in the walls where cannons once stood. There were two or three houses within the fort, and we wondered how people could stand to live shut up within the fort's walls.

When we lived in Detroit two years we moved into a house on Jefferson Avenue where we had a fine view of the river. One day I saw a **sturgeon** so large that the fishermen who had caught it could not get it into their boat. They had to tow it through the water. I had never seen a sturgeon before, and I was quite sure it was a whale!

I never tired of watching the sailboats as they sailed up and down the beautiful river. I watched as Canadian women brought loads of fruits and vegetables in their canoes. Every pleasant evening in the summer happy parties of people rowed up and down the river. They greeted each other and sometimes raced with each other in fun. Just as the sun disappeared, a song would rise

sturgeon - a type of large fish that was once plentiful in the Great Lakes

STURGEON

from the people in some canoe and others would soon join in singing. One song would follow another, until it became too dark and the happy-hearted singers went to their homes.

3

A Maple Sugaring Party

Elizabeth Fisher Baird was born in 1810 at a trading post in Wisconsin, but spent some of her childhood years on Mackinac Island in northern Michigan. At the age of fourteen she married and returned to Wisconsin to live. Mrs. Baird was well educated and wrote down many of her memories about Mackinac Island and Wisconsin Territory. In this story she tells about the fun of maple sugaring on Bois Blanc Island near Mackinac.

I made the trip to Bois Blanc in my dog-sled with my companion, Francois Lacroix. The ride over the ice, across the lake, was a delightful one. The drive through the woods, which had little underbrush, was also charming.

There were many things to do at the sugar camp. I liked playing in the great trees that had been uprooted by wind storms. Near the end of each season, people would come over from Mackinac Island for parties.

One time five ladies and five men came to our camp. Each lady brought a frying pan to fix French crepes, or pancakes. Preparing the batter and the frying pans was a special skill, as was the cooking. They cooked a crepe on one side, tossed it in the air and expected it to land back in the pan in such a way as to cook the other side.

Never did I see objects miss their mark so completely. Crepes flew everywhere but where they were wanted.

Many fell into the fire. Some went to the ground, and one even went over the head of a turner. One gentleman held out his nice fur cap to one of the ladies. He said, "Now turn your cake and I will catch it." This lady was skillful, and before the gentleman knew what had happened she had landed it in his hat. You can imagine what sport we had.

We prepared a nice dinner at the party. We had partridges roasted on sticks before the fire, and rabbit and stuffed squirrel fixed in French fashion. Finally, we had as many crepes with maple syrup as we desired. Every one left the party with sugar cakes and a container of wax, or sugar-gum.

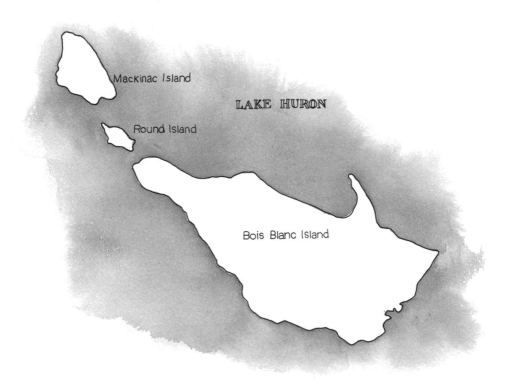

4
Emily's Adventure

Emily Ward came to Michigan with her father in 1822 when she was twelve years old. They settled at Yankee Point on the St. Clair River where Mr. Ward's brother owned land and had a trading business. Later they were joined by Emily's three younger brothers and sisters. (Emily's mother had died when Emily was nine years old.) In the late 1800s a woman named Frances B. Hurlburt collected stories from Emily Ward's life and published them in a book called **Grandmother's Stories.**

One June day after dinner, I decided to go over to the Canadian side of the St. Clair River to a place that was thick with wild strawberries. I did not go alone, but took my cousins Sallie and little Bobbie and a girl named Margaret who worked for Sallie's family. We crossed the river in a rowboat and then pulled it high up on the beach so that the waves would not carry it away. We had a good time filling our pails and baskets with fine fruit.

When we finished picking berries we were tired and walked slowly back to the boat. But little Bobby was still full of energy and went skipping ahead of us. When we were almost to the beach he came running back to us, yelling "boaty, boaty!"

I knew in a moment that he had done some mischief. I set my strawberries down and ran as fast as I could to the river. Sure enough. Bobby had pushed the boat into the water and sent it floating away in the river's current. I waded clear out to my neck, but I could not reach it. Because I could not swim I could not go on but had to wade back to shore.

When I returned Margaret, Sallie, and Bobby all began to cry. We were miles from any houses. We thought we would have to sleep in the the woods where wolves and bears still roamed. I tried to think of what we could do. There was an island about a mile downriver from us, and I believed the river's current would carry the boat there. But how could we get to the island?

I looked around the beach and found some driftwood of logs and some long poles that pioneers use in building mud-chimneys. I thought we could build a raft with these if we could tie them together. But what would we use for strings? I decided we could use our sunbonnets, aprons, dresses, and skirts to tie the logs. I told the girls my plan, and they didn't believe it could be done. But they helped me build the raft, because it seemed to be our only way to get home.

You may be sure that the raft we built was a frail one to be sailing on the great waters of the St. Clair River. Sallie said she was sure we would drown. Since the raft was large enough for only two, Margaret and I went. Sallie stayed on the beach to take care of Bobby. All of us

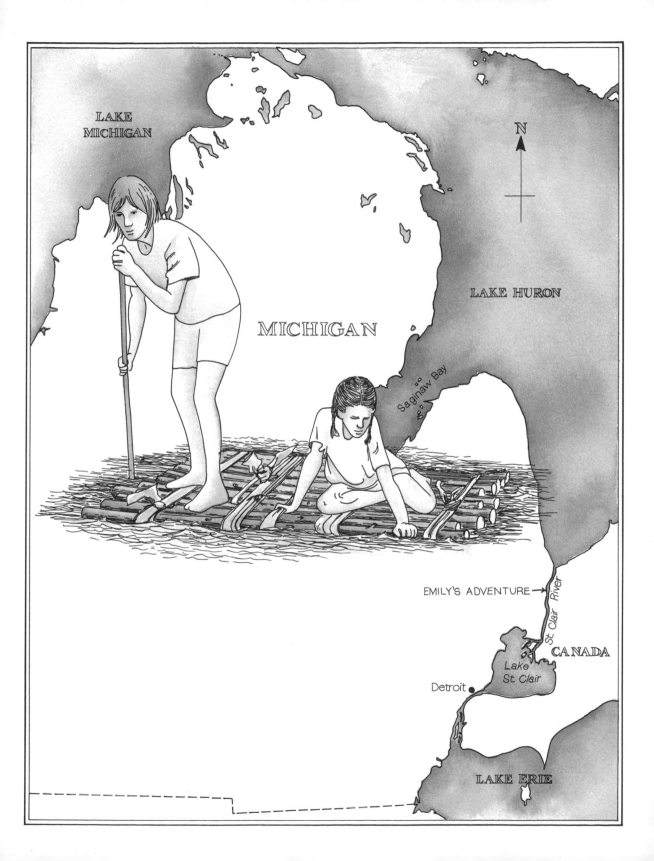

LAKE
MICHIGAN

MICHIGAN

N

LAKE HURON

Saginaw Bay

EMILY'S ADVENTURE →

St. Clair River

CANADA

Lake
St Clair

Detroit ●

LAKE ERIE

had to be brave. Sallie and Bobby had to listen to the howl of a wolf in the distance. The raft we were going to ride on looked as if it would fall to pieces at any moment.

Our plan was to stand on the raft and push and guide it with a pole. But as soon as we moved away from the shore, Margaret was afraid to stand up. She sat down and cried while I did the work. The current moved us along quickly, and soon we could see the island. We knew there was a group of Indians camping there, but we were not afraid of them.

By the time we neared the island the moon was up. We could see Indians on the shore looking in our direction. As we got nearer and nearer and the bright moonlight shone on us, they discovered we were only two frightened girls on a crazy raft. They screamed and shouted with laughter. I didn't care for that, but I did see our little rowboat had landed further down the shore and I knew that soon our troubles would be over.

The Indians were very kind to us. The men untied the raft and gave us back our wet clothes. Then they went up the shore to rescue our rowboat. The women took us to a wigwam and helped us wring out our clothes and put them back on. Then they all helped us into the rowboat and pushed us off with friendly goodbyes. I quickly rowed back to rescue Sallie and Bobby.

Sallie and Bobby jumped up and down with joy when we got back to them. They quickly climbed into the boat and we started for home. We slipped into the house the back way and did not tell anyone about our adventure. It was a long time before our families found out. By then no one was angry or frightened, but only laughed as they passed the story along to others.

5
Settling in Michigan

The following story is taken from the writing of Mr. A. D. P. Van Buren of Battle Creek. Mr. Van Buren came to Michigan from New York State in 1836 when he was a young boy. Later in his life he wrote about his family's journey here and described pioneer life.

On October 1, 1836, my parents, my sister and I, with our household goods, left our home in Oneida County, New York. We boarded a canal boat to take us to Buffalo on the Erie Canal. Some weeks' travel brought us to Buffalo. Here we took a a new steamer, the *United States,* and made a speedy trip on Lake Erie to Detroit. The boat was crowded with people. Most of them planned to start new homes in the West.

My father had visited Michigan a year before our trip and bought some land. Then in the spring of 1836 he sent my two older brothers there to build a log house. As we stepped off the steamer in Detroit, we found one of my brothers, Ephraim, waiting for us. He had come from Calhoun County, a trip of 125 miles, with a wagon and two yoke of oxen to take us to our new home.

We left Detroit and traveled along a wagon track which wound through the forest lands of Wayne County. It seemed to us the worst road that anyone could ever travel. As the oxen walked slowly through the deep woods, we felt sad about leaving our home in New York. It was hard to be excited about traveling to a new place to live.

At dusk we stopped at a **rude** log cabin along the road. Outside the cabin was a rough sign which said, "J. Dow—Entertainment." This was the **tavern** sign. The couple who owned the cabin said they had room for us to stay for the night.

The tired oxen were unyoked and put into a shed made of logs. They were given **marsh hay** and corn. We were taken into the cabin, which had only one room and an attic. Then we were fed wheat bread, butter, boiled potatoes, fried pork, pickles, and tea.

When it was time for bed, my brother and I climbed a ladder into the loft. There was a bed made of rough hickory poles. The bottom of the bed was woven with

34

rude - roughly built.

tavern - a place where travelers could eat, drink, and sleep.

marsh hay - a rough grass from marshes or swamps used to make a poor type of hay.

tick - a mattress cover, sometimes called a bedtick.

smaller hickory poles and covered with a cotton **tick** filled with a little hay. We also had a sheet and a quilt or two. To sleep on such a bed, we had to be very tired, which we were.

We awoke in the morning feeling sore all over. We had marks on our sides and backs from those **hickory** poles. The next morning we ate breakfast and my father paid the bill. It was fifty cents a meal, twenty-five cents for the beds, and fifty cents for the oxen's hay and corn.

We found the road on our second day to be even worse than the first road. Once our wagon sunk into mud so deep we could not get it out. Finally another group of settlers came along, and they hitched their oxen to ours. By doubling the oxen power, our wagon was pulled out. We found settlers to be helpful and friendly on our trip.

Along the road we found signs that other travelers had also had trouble. There were poles and rails, used as levers to lift wagons out of mud holes. Sometimes we saw pieces of wagons, such as broken wheels. In some places stagecoaches had been wrecked and left to rot.

At sunset on the second day we came to Plymouth. It was a pretty village with a beautiful green lawn at its center. A church stood at one end of the town, and a tavern at the other end. We spent the night at this tavern. There were also other groups of travelers there. After supper we all talked about our experiences and our plans for the future. Since settling in Michigan was on everyone's mind, we became friends easily.

Leaving Plymouth on the third day we traveled in a southwesterly direction. There were several inns along

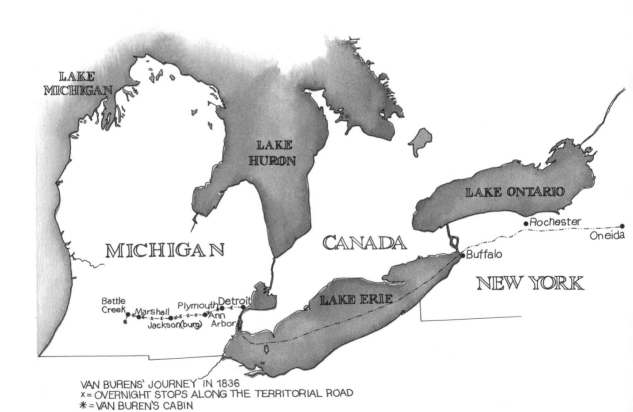

VAN BURENS' JOURNEY IN 1836
x = OVERNIGHT STOPS ALONG THE TERRITORIAL ROAD
✳ = VAN BUREN'S CABIN

the way. Twelve miles from Plymouth we stopped at Dixborough. We stayed at an inn crowded with people who were also moving to Michigan. After supper we went into a crowded room where people were gathered around a tub of water. A man asked people to put their hands in the tub. Someone did and jerked out his hand with a yell. Another person tried and also yelled. The room was filled with laughter, and everyone was very curious. Finally the man took a tool and pulled a strange creature out of the water. It was an **electric eel** which sends out shocks.

Electric eel - a strange type of fish that gives electric shocks. This eel comes from South America and would not have been caught from a Michigan lake or river. Perhaps the man had bought it to entertain people.

oak openings - open areas in oak forests where the trees grew so tall and gave so much shade that little else could grow beneath them.

corduroy roads - roads made of logs

CORDUROY ROAD

We continued our journey across southern Michigan on the Territorial Road. We stayed near Ann Arbor. From there the road was better. There were **oak openings** with fewer mud holes. There were bridges on the rivers and streams. Sections of **corduroy roads** had been built over some of the worst marshes. No one rode on the wagon but my mother and sister. Sometimes they walked when we came to difficult places or when they were tired of riding. We stopped at Grass Lake and Jacksonburg.

The next day on our journey my mother fell from the wagon and was hurt. This was some two miles east of Sandstone near Beck's tavern. We stayed at the tavern on account of the accident, but left the next day. There was a long stretch of corduroy road over a black marsh. Before the corduroy road was built, we were told, horses often could not walk across it. To keep from sinking they had to be rolled over and over again until they reached harder ground.

We traveled on and spent our nights at inns. We stopped near Parma, at Graham's tavern near Albion, and at Colonel Maynard's inn near Marshall. In the last two days of travel we left the Territorial Road. We crossed a **prairie** and drove two miles further into a woods. Then we stopped before a new log house. It was to be our

---

prairie - a large area of grassland with few or no trees. Michigan had small prairies scattered in the southwestern area. Pioneers quickly settled on these prairies where they did not have to cut trees to begin farming.

---

home in Michigan. We looked around us for neighbors, but there was nothing but oak openings. We were alone in the silent woods.

A home in the woods

Our new home was completely in the woods. Out of doors was beautiful, wild Michigan. You could see through the trees in any direction, except where there were hills. You could walk, ride on horseback, or drive in a wagon wherever you pleased in these woods. You were as free as you could be in a neat and beautiful park.

There were no roads or fences, but only trails worn deep by Indians. From the door of our log house we could often see long files of Indians, on foot and on ponies, making their way along these trails. At first our only visitors were animals. Deer often fed near the cabin. At night we sometimes heard the howl of a lone wolf. Now and then a bear would try to attack our pigs, or a fox would kill one of our chickens.

We soon learned about the forest around us. There were twelve different kinds of oak trees. One of them, the burr oak, had an acorn that was good for feeding to hogs. There were black walnut trees, that were valuable for building cabinets. They also bore large nuts that were good to eat. In addition to the black walnut trees, were hickory, butternut, beechnut, and hazelnut trees, all with good nuts to eat.

Throughout the woods there were grapevines hanging from trees. We saw large thickets of blackberry bushes. And we were told that in the spring the openings were fairly red with large and delicious strawberries. Wild plum trees grew along the small streams, while huckleberries and cranberries grew in the marshes.

Once we were in our new home, we had to find a way to make a living. Like most pioneers, our money was gone by the time we reached our land and built a cabin. My brothers had cut hay for the cattle from a marsh nearby. But we needed corn for the pigs and hens. We also needed winter food supplies for the family. We worked husking corn and digging potatoes in trade for supplies, but many things were scarce and could not be bought or traded.

The first year was a discouraging time for us. There was no wheat, and we had only cornbread. There were few hogs, and pork was scarce. There was little beef because there were few cows in the country. Those had to be used for milk or sometimes to work beside an ox. Sometimes we would kill a deer and have venison to eat. My father had brought five hundred pounds of codfish from New York. When possible, we traded fish to our neighbors for pork. This trading was called "paying in dicker."

Mixing up feed for the chickens

When we first came to this state we were told that we would get the "Michigan appetite" after we had lived here for a short time. We found this to be true. It seemed that all we worked for was to get enough to eat. But we could never get ahead since we were hungry all the time!

The settlers' food supplies were wheat, corn, pork, and potatoes. Families often went without meat except for the game they could kill. Salt was also scarce at times, and once was as high as twenty-one dollars a barrel. We rarely had tea, coffee, sugar, or butter. An herb called tea-weed was used by some settlers. We often had crust coffee which was made from roasted wheat or other grain.

Our usual meal was made up of a platter of boiled potatoes, bread or Johnny cake, and sometimes meat. We ate a lot of gravy made from flour, water, salt, and flavored with a little meat if we had it. Nothing but dishes was left after the meal.

One Sunday morning I was home alone. Always hungry, I thought about making something to eat. Luckily I found some flour, lard, and salt. I was delighted and went to work to make shortcake. I had seen my mother and sister make this, and I thought I could make it myself. So, rolling up my sleeves, I went to work.

I mixed up the flour and water, put in a little lard and salt, and kneaded away. Finally, it seemed to me to be ready for the pan. But you should have seen my hands! The dough hung in strings from my fingers. Just as I rolled out the cake and put it in the pan, I heard a rap at the door. Frightened, I put the cake in a **spider** to bake over warm coals in the fireplace and answered the door.

spider - a frying pan. Early frying pans had legs so that they could stand above the coals in the fireplace.

It was a young man, Uriah Herson, who had come a long way to see my older brothers. He wanted to shake my hand, but I said it was doughy because I was making chicken feed. I told him my family had gone to a church meeting at the local schoolhouse. During this time I tried to block the doorway so that he could not look in and see that I was baking.

Suddenly, there was the yelp—yelp—yelp of a chicken. Looking around I saw a young rooster with both feet stuck in my shortcake dough. He stood there with his wings stretched out and his bill full of dough, making all sorts of sounds. Uriah looked in at the table and fireplace and saw the whole mess. He said he guessed he would go

to the church meeting and find my family. Then he went off laughing at my chicken pie.

When Uriah left, I quickly raced to my shortcake. I pulled the chicken out and flung him out the door. Then I took a knife and cut out the middle of the cake that he had jumped in. I smoothed over the rest of the cake and returned it to bake over the fireplace coals.

Meanwhile, the drama of the shortcake was still going on outside. The other chickens crowded around the rooster and picked the dough off his legs and feet. They went after the shortbread dough so wildly that the rooster's feet and legs began to bleed. I drove off the greedy group, and the rooster hobbled away on his half-baked feet.

Once more by the fireplace, I watched my cake bake. Then I made a square meal on that shortcake. There was none left, so my mother would not find out what I'd done. This adventure remained a secret for a long time. It finally got out. Uriah, no doubt, thought the story was too good to keep to himself. I told the story to my family in my own way—mixing up feed for the chickens.

Raisings, logging bees, husking bees, quilting bees and many other activities with the word "bee" meant a gathering of settlers to get a job done for a neighbor. It was a union of workers to help one pioneer family do what it could not do alone. Thus, pioneers built their houses and barns, husked their corn, or did their logging with one another's help. In the evening they sang songs and enjoyed one another's company.

When cabins were few and far between, it was hard to invite your neighbors to a bee. A pioneer would walk miles to let the neighbors know he needed help. However, he knew that his neighbors would always be ready to join in the work.

Houseraisings

A pioneer usually had the logs cut before neighbors arrived to raise the house. The raising began when the men carefully placed two logs where the sides of the cabin would be. Then they put two more logs where the front and back of the cabin would be. They had to be sure the base of the cabin was straight and sturdy. Four good axmen were placed at each of the corners where the logs

44

met. Their job was to cut a notch at the end of the logs so that they would fit together snugly.

Once the frame was made, other logs could be added more quickly. The axmen notched each log before the others lifted it in place. As the walls began to rise, the job became harder. The men made ramps to help them roll, push, or pull the logs into place.

When the walls were high enough, the men began to make the roof. At the two ends of the cabin they built gables, or the upper parts of a house that comes to a peak. They put up rafters and a long ridgepole to support the gables and roof. Roof coverings were made of hay, bark, or wide strips of wood called shakes.

The pioneers cut holes in the new cabin to make windows and a door. They filled the cracks in the walls with small pieces of wood, clay, and mud. Some pioneers used the ground as a cabin floor, but others split logs and smoothed the flat side to make a floor. Chimneys were built of sticks which were put together much like the cabin walls. Pioneers plastered the inside of the chimney with clay to keep it from catching on fire.

Potawatomi Indians helped pioneers at houseraisings in the southwestern part of the state. I know of a time where only two white men were at a raising. The rest were Indians. They lifted cheerfully and rolled the logs with great strength.

Splitting rails

Rail splitting was important when pioneers were clearing the land and building fences. A regular rail splitter could cut and split about one hundred rails in a day. A good hand could split about two hundred a day. The wages were one dollar for a hundred rails or fifty cents plus room and board for a hundred rails. My two brothers split rails during the winter of

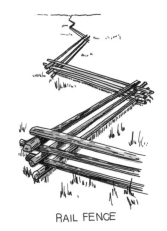

RAIL FENCE

1837. They split fifteen thousand rails for one man and eight thousand for another. The tools they used for their work were a beetle, iron wedges, and an ax.

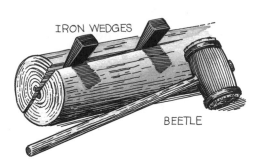

Breaking up

Some settlers had a regular job breaking up—or plowing land for the first time. The prairies were hardest to break since the roots of grass and weeds were very thick. The soil where tall oak trees had been cut was the easiest to plow.

A settler who had a job breaking up needed six or seven yoke of oxen. He had to be strong to hold a breaking-up plow behind the oxen. He also had to work his team around stones, stumps, and trees.

Settlers who had jobs breaking up, earned five dollars an acre for their work. After a day's work they had to take their plows to a blacksmith's shop to be sharpened. Many had to travel six to ten miles to a shop.

Husking bees

Husking bees in our area were not like those in the East where both boys and girls attended. Only settlers

47

and their sons attended these. We had fun, and we also got work done.

Husking bees were not always the same. Sometimes a pile of corn was put into two parts and teams were chosen to husk against each other. These were lively, noisy races. Other times we would all sing. Another entertainment at husking bees was storytelling. We had few books to read, but we told their stories over and over again to each other.

6

A Fight With Walter & Other School Memories

In the fall of 1837 Mr. McCormick of Flint sent his son, W. R. McCormick, to a school in Saginaw. W. R. lived with a Major Mosley who lived in a fort there. The boy did chores in the morning and evening to earn his meals and a place to sleep. Much later in his life he wrote about a fight he had with another student, Walter Cronk.

Our teacher was Horace S. Beach, a kind-hearted man and a good teacher. He had a lot of boys who were hard to deal with, but he knew how to solve problems. I remember how he solved a problem I had one day with Walter Cronk.

While we were in the classroom, Walter and I had a argument. Walter said he would whip me when school let out for nooning. So while going out the door, Walter gave me a kick and sent me tumbling down the icy steps. This made me mad, and at it we went.

Walter was really a bigger and better fighter than I was. But I happened to get hold of his neckerchief, and before I knew it, I gave him two black eyes. He got me down after that and was pounding me when Mr. Beach stopped us and told us we would settle this after dinner.

When I got back to school after dinner, I found Walter already there. He was ashamed of his black eyes and had not gone home to eat. While we waited for Mr. Beach, we made up and became friends.

When Mr. Beach came back he had five good-sized branches over his shoulder. The other boys yelled that we were going to get it, but we already knew that. We watched while Mr. Beach sat down and began carefully trimming the branches into whips. I looked at Walter, and he looked at me. We knew our time had come.

"Boys, step forward," Mr. Beach said. "I want to settle this little problem." He wanted to know what we had to say and why we should not be punished. I said I did not think I ought to be punished, for I did not start the fight. Walter, whose eyes were so swollen he could hardly see, said he had been punished enough.

"Well," Mr. Beach said, "I have a proposition to make. You see these whips and you see those six cords of maple wood at the door. You can cut that wood at recess and noon-times or settle things now."

I did not like the idea of settling things now. I had tried that before, so I said I would cut the wood. At first Walter said he would like to settle things now. But when Mr. Beach raised the whip, Walter changed his mind.

At recess that afternoon Walter and I started our job on the six cords of wood. I sawed and Walter split, and all the other boys stood and laughed at us.

Not long after our fight, my father called me home for spring work. One day I came back to Saginaw and stopped by the school. There was Walter still sawing wood. He said he had jumped the job three or four times, but every time he had got a whipping. Finally he decided to finish it up.

Walter and I have been, and continue to be, the best of friends ever since our schoolboy fight nearly forty years ago.

C. B. Seymour grew up near Ann Arbor. These are the memories he had of his school days.

My first schooling in Michigan was in my father's house. One of my older sisters was the teacher. My next school was in Dexter village, two and half miles away. This was the winter after I was seven years old. The children of Mr. Roberts, one of our neighbors, attended this school all one winter. Many times we walked through snow deeper than we could well manage, and it was almost dark before we reached their home. Then I had to go on walking some distance before I reached my house. My feet carried me lively during that last part of the trip. Often I heard wolves howling in the distance.

The next summer a log schoolhouse was built about two miles from our house. I went there the following winter. Then a schoolhouse was built on my father's farm, and I studied there until I was sixteen or seventeen. I went to school a few months in the winter and worked on the farm long months in the spring and summer.

An academy was started in Ann Arbor, and my father rented a room for me there. The room had a bed, a small table, a chair, and a stove. Every Monday morning I left home for this room in Ann Arbor. I took food which my mother prepared and it lasted me a whole week. I went to this school a part of a winter, and this was my college training.

In those days schoolroom furniture was rather limited. We had no easy seats with backs, or desks in front of us for our books. We held our books in our hands while studying. When we had to do our arithmetic on slates, our hands had all they could do.

Our seats were slabs sawed from logs, with holes in them for stakes or legs for them to stand on. These benches usually stretched the whole length of the room on each side. Students sat on them in rows like birds on a fence. The boys sat on one side of the room, and the girls sat on the other side.

Our desks for writing were boards whose edges also served as backs to our seats. When it came time for our

STUDENTS SAT IN ROWS, THE GIRLS ON ONE SIDE, THE BOYS ON THE OTHER

writing lessons, we would whirl around and throw our feet over the seat. (Our pens were made from the quills of our own chickens.) When the lesson was finished w e would whirl back again, ready for the next exercise.

The teachers in these schools had a hard job. If they were men, they also had to sweep the floors and keep the fire burning in the stove. If they were women, the older boys would help with these jobs. But both men and women teachers had to rise early in the morning and face a cold schoolhouse. Often we had only green wood to burn, and there was more smoke than heat in the classroom.

Even though the schoolhouse was not comfortable, it was the center of public gatherings of many kinds. Taking candles with us, we gathered in the school in the evening for singing or spelling bees. We had as much fun as the young people today (1890s) who have fancy heated schoolrooms with electric lights.

QUILL PEN

7
Thanksgiving at Yankee Springs

Mrs. Mary Hoyt was a young girl when her family settled in southwestern Michigan about halfway between the present cities of Grand Rapids and Kalamazoo . Later in her life she wrote a history of the Yankee Springs area and described Thanksgiving at the tavern run by her family.

The first Thanksgiving celebrated at Yankee Springs tavern was in the fall of 1838. My father sent out invitations to all the new settlers for miles around. Later he sent men with wagons and teams of horses to gather them in. My mother meanwhile directed the first Thanksgiving dinner in the new country. It was made up of wild turkeys brought by the Indians from the Gun Lake woods and two huge pieces of spare ribs. Both the turkeys and the ribs were roasted over a great open fireplace. My mother made mince pies, pumpkin pies, and puddings in a large brick oven by the kitchen fireplace. The Indians brought cranberries, which was the only fall berry. No fruit tree or berry bush had yet been planted.

The tables were spread and the guests came from their homes in the woods to enjoy this feast prepared for them in such a fine way. The guests must have thought about the homes, families, and friends they had left in order to settle in Michigan, but they did not mourn. Instead they enjoyed the feast and were thankful for it.

It began to snow, the first snow of the season, but the harder it snowed, the livelier the party became. An old violin was pulled out of some corner and all began dancing. They kept dancing until morning when breakfast was prepared for them. The guests were then taken back to their homes. So passed our first Thanksgiving at Yankee Springs.

8
A Boy's Story of Pioneer Life

When Theodore E. Potter was fourteen years old, his father died on the farm they were clearing near Eaton Rapids. Theodore's mother was left with the job of raising a family of seven children whose ages ranged from three to seventeen years of age. Since she had moved fifteen times in her married life, she refused to leave their new farm as long as her children lived at home and could help with the work.

The following adventures that happened in 1846 are taken from Theodore Potter's writing, "A Boy's Story of Pioneer Life." They include a story about a deer attacking him, which seems strange to us today. However, bucks will sometimes attack people, and there are several accounts of deer attacks in the letters and journals of Michigan pioneers.

I was but fourteen years old. We were living in a log shanty. My father had died only a month before, leaving my mother with seven children, three cows, one yoke of oxen, and seven acres of cleared land.

My oldest brother was eighteen and the youngest was three. There were no schools near us and only a few settlers in the township. Our cows, with bells on, ran free in the woods. In stormy weather they often stayed out overnight and it was my duty to find them early in the morning.

One day I started out with my younger brother and a small dog. We could hear the bells about a mile away. As we came in sight of the cows, the dog began to bark at a large buck deer with great antlers. The animals began to fight, and I went forward to help the dog. The deer forgot the dog and went after me. I ran behind a big black oak tree. When the deer would start to attack me, the dog would snap at his heels. My little brother stood looking on, frightened and screaming at the top of his voice.

I was able to reach a dry oak limb which I used as a club. Whenever the deer would try to attack me, I would hit him on the head. Finally I knocked him down and pounded him on the head until he was dead. My brother came up and we tried to drag the animal home, but he was too heavy. In our excitement we forgot all about the cows and started for home on the run to carry the news to the family.

We found our oldest brother at home with two men who were helping him do some work. We told them what we had done, but it was hard to get them to believe it. They finally decided to go with us and see for themselves. They found that our story was true and that the buck was a very large one. They dressed it, and then we all returned home with plenty of meat for the family for a whole week.

The story of my fight with the deer was published in our county newspaper. It was copied by Detroit newspapers, calling it a great deed for a boy of fourteen. My mother told me that from that time on I should have a gun to carry whenever I went after the cows.

For the first time in my life I was permitted to hunt with a gun. There was a gun in our family that had been used in the **Revolutionary War** and in the **War of 1812**. This was my first gun, and I felt real proud of it. Whenever I went into the woods, this historic gun was with me. The same month I killed the deer with a club, I shot at no less than five deer and missed every one. My mother said to me, "Ted, if you expect to supply the family with **venison**, you had better trade your gun off for a dry oak limb."

Revolutionary War - fought between the American colonies and Great Britain from 1775 to 1781. It made the colonies a free nation called the United States of America.

War of 1812 - fought between the United States and Great Britain from 1812 to 1814. It settled arguments about the boundaries between the United States and Canada.

Venison - deer meat

That fall word came to us that a bear was killing the hogs of a neighbor named Jones who lived about two miles away. They wanted me and my older brother to come at once with our guns and lanterns. When we got there we found the bear had broken the back of one of the hogs and had been chased away by Mrs. Jones and her dogs. We knew the bear was still nearby, because the dogs kept howling.

We killed the hog and told Mrs. Jones to take the dogs to the house and shut them up. Then we dragged the hog to a log bridge about ten feet high and hid behind a nearby tree. My brother thought of this plan, claiming that the bear was hungry and would follow the hog where we dragged it to the bridge. We took our position lower than the bridge so we could look up toward the sky and see the bear if he came on the bridge.

We had not been waiting more than thirty minutes before the bear appeared on the bridge. He must have smelled us and become fearful. He looked down on us and my brother whispered, "Now is our time, take aim—fire." We did and the bear made a jump, landing about six feet from us. He then began running, smashing into the top of a fallen tree, making terrific groans, and breaking and chewing the limbs.

Not knowing what would happen next, we climbed on the bridge and lit our lanterns. We were prepared to fight it out with the bear. But others had heard our shots. Another neighbor, Tile Cogswell, fired three shots to let us know he was on his way with his bear dogs. Others passed the signal that there was trouble by ringing cowbells or blowing horns. Soon about twenty men were on the bridge with us, listening to the groans of the bear.

Tile Cogswell let his dogs loose, and we all followed with lanterns and guns. We found the bear so badly wounded he could not run, but he did fight with the dogs. He killed one of the dogs, while another dog was killed by a shot meant for the bear. Then Tile Cogswell ran forward to save the rest of his dogs and shot the bear in the head.

We then decided to go to my house and get my mother's ox-team. With the oxen we dragged the bear to our place that night and dressed it. We planned a holiday for the next day, so all the neighbors within five miles could have a share of the largest black bear ever killed in that part of the state. He weighed nearly four hundred pounds.

It was a great relief to all the settlers around to know that this bear was dead. He had been killing hogs in the township for two years. It was found that both my brother and I hit the bear, and that either of the shots would have killed him sooner or later. My brother told me that I should do my hunting after dark, since I had not been able to hit much in the daytime.

Early Train Rides

Mortimer A. Leggett came to Michigan from New York City. Over fifty years later he wrote about coming to Michigan and taking the railroad to what was then the town of Pontiac.

In 1852 my father and his family left the city of New York for the, then Far West, as Michigan was called. We sailed up the Hudson River to Albany. From Albany we went to Buffalo on the New York Central Railroad, then a single track. From Buffalo we took a steamboat for Detroit, as there were no railroads out from Buffalo.

From Detroit we went on to Pontiac by train. We boarded the much-talked-of railroad that ran on the strap-rail. The train had a very small engine. It had no tender, or place to hold wood and water.

Two small cars, a baggage and passenger coach, were hitched onto the engine. The passenger car had wooden seats with leather straps for the back. Its windows were so high that one had to stand to look out.

The railroad track was made of square timbers along the bed, much like the steps in a ladder. At the edge of these timbers was a thin, flat iron strap. The tracks soon became very rough, and sometimes the two little driving wheels of the engine would get caught in the hollows in the rails. When that happened the passengers had to get out and help pull the engine out.

I found there were other jobs for the passengers of this train. On one hill the engine could not pull the cars up the grade, so passengers had to put their shoulders to the wheels and help it up. Sometimes the passengers had to go into the woods and pick up wood to burn in the steam engine to keep the train running.

When we came into Pontiac it was both an exciting and confusing time. The train pulled into a building which had two open ends. The freight was unloaded on one side of the train, while we stepped out on the other side. We were met by the noisy criers, each yelling that their tavern was the best place to stay. There were also criers telling us about stagecoaches that ran to Flint, Saginaw, or other towns.

Pontiac at this time was a small place that became busy and crowded at times during the year. It was a center where farmers brought in their produce. In the wheat season the streets would be lined with teams. It was a common sight to see a farmer going to town with a yoke of oxen hitched to a farm wagon. He would have his family with him and in the back part of his wagon would be bags of wheat that they used to pay their bills. The country taverns did a great business in those days, since people would be away from home about three days and needed places to stay and food to eat.

Other pioneers in Michigan also remembered the early railroads. Mrs. Mary Hoyt, who told about her first Thanksgiving in Michigan, also wrote about her first railroad ride from Battle Creek to Detroit.

We lived in Yankee Springs ten years before the Michigan Central Railway was built nearby. We kept hearing that it was being built, but it took so long that the old stagecoach kept running for many years. The building of the railroad began in Detroit in 1836 when Michigan was a territory. It was finished to Kalamazoo in 1846. Six years later, in 1852, the line ran all the way to Chicago.

My first ride on the railroad came at a time when my father represented the counties of Allegan and Barry in the State Legislature in 1846. He came home for a short time during the winter, and when he returned, my sister and I went with him for a two-week stay in the capital city.

The ride to Battle Creek was in a stagecoach pulled by four horses. From Battle Creek we took our first and never-to-be-forgotten ride on that new railroad we had heard so much about. We were nearly frightened to death with the almost constant scream of the engine whistle and the clanking of the cars over the rough road. We wished ourselves back in the old stagecoach many times before the journey ended.

C. B. Seymore tells about a train ride he took in 1840 from Ann Arbor to Detroit. The ride was part of a big rally held just before the election for President of the United States. Mr. Seymore clearly wanted William Henry Harrison to beat Martin Van Buren, and he did!

A celebration was to be held in Detroit, the final grand "blow out" before the election. The Michigan Central Railroad, built as far west as Ann Arbor, was to run a train from Ann Arbor to Detroit. The train was to leave at four o'clock. Our party walked to Ann Arbor, but found, to our great disappointment, that the train would not leave until the next morning at eight o'clock. Some of us walked back six miles to the house of one of our company to spend the night.

We got up the next morning at four o'clock to make sure we would not miss the train. We found a rain storm in full force, but it did not dampen our spirits. We said that any rain was better than the reign of Martin Van Buren!

When we arrived at the station we found all of the passenger and box cars filled with people. We climbed on an open flat car. There we stood in the rain all the way to Detroit.

Recently, I took a little journey on the Michigan Central Railroad. It was magnificent, with a dining room and sleeping car. I could not help but think of that trip over fifty years ago. Railroad cars then had plain wooden seats. The track was only a single one with a flat bar of iron on top. But I thought, even as I stood in the rain, that it was fast and modern compared to the team of oxen that had brought us to Michigan thirteen years before. Such is the progress of mankind!

1 0

Where the Birds Sang First in Spring

Elizabeth Whitney Williams was born on Mackinac Island. Her mother had been married to a Frenchman until he died and left her with three boys. She then married Walter Whitney, Elizabeth's father.

When Elizabeth was a young child, she lived with her family on a little island in northern Lake Michigan called St. Helena Island. There her father helped build a large ship. When that job was done, the family moved to Manistique where Mr. Whitney was hired to work in a mill. They then moved to Beaver Island, where they lived for many years.

Elizabeth Whitney Williams had a long and interesting life. She wrote her life story in a book called **A Child of the Sea; and Life Among the Mormons.** *One of the stories in her book takes place during the brief time the family moved to and lived in Manistique. There her parents took in a distant relative who had been a fur trader for years and who spoke little English. Elizabeth and her brothers quickly learned to love the old man, whom they called Grandpa. They also adored his old dog, Bob.*

This story begins as the family moves from St. Helena Island to Manistique. They stop at a place called Scott Point, where people came to earn a living by fishing in the summer. They would then leave the area in the late fall. The story shows Elizabeth's family caring deeply about the people and animals in their lives.

Father decided to take our own little boat, the "Abbigail," to Manistique. If we went on a larger boat, we would not be able to take our pets. Sailors thought it was bad luck to move cats from place to place. But we had cats, dogs, rabbits and sea gulls for pets, and father would not leave any of them behind. Our goods were all loaded on the "Nancy" and the "Abbigail." I remember our neighbors coming to the beach to see us off. Father took me and placed me in the boat, where brother Charley and I were wrapped in warm blankets. Our boat was pushed off by the men who said, "God bless you, Whitney," and then waved their hats and handkerchiefs. We sailed away on the blue waters of Lake Michigan.

The time had now come when the people of this little settlement were to pack and go to their winter homes. They were to leave all their fishing outfits locked in their buildings until they came again another year. Our family stood on the shore to wave goodbye, and they sailed to their far-away homes for the winter.

A family who remained there were an old couple named McWilliams with a young son of seventeen years. The couple felt the trip was too long for them to take, so they wanted to stay there all winter. They chose a place called Birch Point, a cold bleak shore where only a few Indian hunters came in the winter.

Our goods had been shipped to Manistique, and we were to follow in our boat. But mother and father did not want to leave the old couple. Mr. McWilliams was sick, and our family stayed for two weeks until he died. Father made the casket, and we buried him on that lonely shore where he once sat and watched the waves roll in on the white sandy beach.

My mother and father tried hard to have the mother and son go with us to Manistique. But they would not leave the grave of their loved one. My parents told me later that it was a great sorrow to leave the mother and son alone. There were many wolves and bears there. At

70

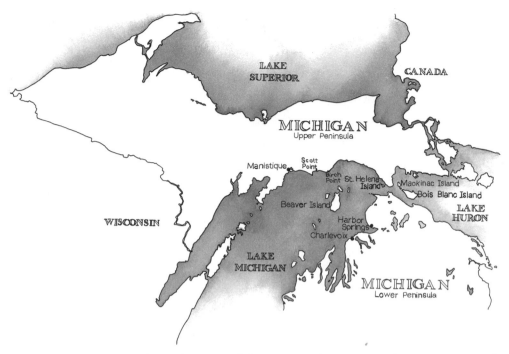

night they would sit outside our doors and snap and growl at each other.

One cold morning in November our boat was prepared and we started to Manistique. Charley and I were again placed in warm blankets. Father and the boys rowed while mother steered. We kept close to the shore. Little brother and I were asleep most of the time. I can remember hearing my father singing old hymns. Mother, too, sang her French songs with the boys. French was our mother's language. Father could not speak it, but understood nearly everything. French and Indian were the languages spoken around the shores of northern Lake Michigan by almost everybody in those days.

When we came to Manistique the man who wanted father to work for him came to meet us. He took us to the house where we would stay, and we built a nice fire in the large stone fireplace. Soon we felt at home.

At Manistique we also met Mother's cousin who was an old man of eighty. He had worked for the Hudson Bay Company and the Great American Fur Company, taking trade goods and furs for trappers. The trappers called him Magazau, meaning "store," since he and his dogs carried a regular store for them.

Now Magazau was too old to work and had no home. Father felt sorry for him and gave him a home with us. Magazu was happy and grateful, but he spoke little English. He spoke French and Spanish well because he had French and Spanish parents. He also spoke Indian. We children were taught to call him Grandpa, and he loved it. He was kind and patient with us and never tired of doing something for our comfort.

Grandpa still had one of his work dogs. Bob was eighteen years old. He was large and powerful, dark brown with darker stripes in color. He had pulled loads so long he was almost blind, and his teeth were almost gone. He was also so stiff it was hard for him to get up on his feet after he laid down.

When Grandpa came he talked to Father in his broken English. "Mr. Whitney," he said, "you take me, you take Bob too. Me can't stay if Bob no stay."

72

The old dog seemed to know what his master was saying. He stood close to his master and looked straight into Father's eyes. Father said, "Yes, Bob can stay too."

Bob had not always been kindly treated. He seemed to be afraid to be in anyone's way. When he saw us petting our dogs, he would slink away with his head down and look sad. The young dogs, too, knew he was a stranger and growled at him and bossed him about. Then poor old Bob would go back of the house and cry and whine sadly.

At last Father could stand it no longer. He gave the order that Bob must not be bothered any more and must have a bed behind the stove. He said no one was ever to speak a cross word to Bob or strike him. Grandpa cried with delight.

Sometimes Bob could not get up alone. Father would lift him up and rub his neck and shoulders where his dog sled collar had once been. Very soon Bob would try to go fast to meet Father when he came into the house. Father would talk to him and rub him, and Bob seemed to understand the kindness.

With care Bob improved and got much smarter. Father had to be away all day to his work. At night when he came home Charley, Bob, and I were always at the door to meet him. Sometimes in the winter evenings when Grandpa would be telling us stories and singing his songs, Charley and I would fall fast asleep curled up on the rug with Bob.

One Sunday when we were dressed in our Sunday suits and Father was reading to us, a knock came on the door. The latch lifted, the door opened, and John McWilliams almost fell into the room. "Come, both of you," he said to my parents. "My mother is dead." Then he sank into a chair and cried as if his heart would break. He would not eat, and very shortly he left to return to the cabin.

My mother rose out of her chair and said to Father, "Come, Walter, we must go." Father did not want her to go, since she had been ill. The snow was deep and it was very cold. But neither Father, Grandpa, nor we crying children could stop her from going.

We were left with Grandpa. I remember Father telling him over and over again to be careful. Bob was also told to watch over us children, which he understood. We were crying and hanging on to our parents when Mother said, "Now listen children. Be good and mind all that Grandpa tells you. Don't you know poor John has no one with him? His mother is dead." We were quiet, but sorrowful.

Mother and Father's trip to the McWilliams' cabin was a difficult one. It was a trip of about fifteen miles, and it began to snow heavily. Mother was tired, but father urged her on, knowing that they must reach a small shanty where they could stay until morning. The snow was deep and the wolves began to howl as dusk set in. Mother worried about us children, and Father worried that someone might have torn down the old shanty and there would be no shelter for the night. When Mother could go no farther, Father left his tools and gun and carried her on his back.

The wolves were right behind them when Father finally reached the shanty. He had to drop Mother to the floor and quickly bar the door. Luckily, someone had left wood stacked near an old stove. There was also a little lantern with fish oil. Soon they were warm and more comfortable. The wolves still howled outside the door, however, and even jumped to the roof. Father

WOLF

wished many times that night that his gun was not back lying in the snow.

The next morning the wolves had left and all was quiet. Mother felt better, and after Father returned with his tools and gun, they went on to the McWilliams cabin where they found John. Then Father built a coffin while Mother cooked and baked for John who refused to leave the cabin until spring. Two Indian hunters came by and helped father dig the grave. Later they brought Mother and Father home on their sleds.

While Mother baked John told her about his family. They had once lived in Canada. His oldest brother was arrested for a crime, and the McWilliams family sold their farm to pay the debt. The boy promised he would do better, and the whole family moved to Michigan where they heard that money could be earned by fishing. They bought a boat and nets and began fishing. But after a short time the older son took the boat and nets, sold them, and never returned with the money.

John said that his brother's action had broken his father's heart. Once his father died, his mother also died of unhappiness. Then John told my parents, "Now I am left alone to battle the world, but I shall never forget your kindnesses to me."

Mother worried about John McWilliams living alone, but the Indians decided to move their families near his cabin until spring. Once he became ill, and they cared for him. When summer came John worked with fishermen.

Then he received word that his uncle in Canada wanted him to live with him. He went with a grateful heart.

While Mother and Father were gone for four days to help John, we had our troubles at home. I cried all night with an earache, and poor Grandpa had his hands full. He was up all night, and he worried about Father and Mother. He was sure they had frozen to death or had been eaten by wolves.

To make things harder, brother Toney went out alone one day to find the rabbit traps he had set. Coming home he lost his way. When he did not come back at dinner time, Grandpa was almost crazy. He would not let brother Lewis go look for him, thinking he might also get lost. Then he left us with Lewis and ran down to the river. There he yelled and swung his arms until the men at the mill heard him. They came over in their boats, but could not understand what Grandpa said. They came to the house, and Lewis told them Toney was lost and Mother and Father were gone.

Soon the men were ready to start a search for Toney. They had dogs with them, but they also wanted Bob. When Bob started to leave with the men, Charley and I cried. Bob heard us and ran back, licking our hands and faces. Then the man put a rope around Bob's neck and led him away.

At first the men could not make Bob understand what they wanted him to do. They could not speak to him in French, which was the language Bob knew best. They let him smell my brother's clothes and shoes, and at last he looked up at them and barked. Then he started with his nose to the ground.

The younger dogs made it difficult for Bob. They jumped over and around him and wanted to play. But Bob had something more important to do. He circled and seemed confused. Then he threw his head up in the air and gave several loud, sharp barks. He looked at the men and seemed to say, "Follow me."

Bob was old, but he left the men far behind even though they went as fast as they could. The men were uneasy because it was getting dark. Suddenly they heard Bob's deep voice barking excitedly. He didn't stop barking until the men reached him. He was standing directly over Toney, who was lying in the snow. Bob had scratched the snow away and had partly dragged him out.

At first the men thought Toney was dead. But he was so terribly tired from walking and being frightened by

the thought of darkness and wolves that he had fallen in the snow and could not get up. The men carried him home, reaching there at ten o'clock at night with the wolves howling after them.

The next day two men from the mill set out to see if Mother and Father were safe. They met them coming back with the Indians. What happy children we were to see them again. Bob was also wild with delight to see Father and Mother. When they learned that Bob had saved Toney's life, there was nothing too good for him.

Grandpa was especially glad to see Mother and Father, because his trials were great with us four children. One day he said to Father in his broken English, "Oh, Mr. Whitney, I so scare. I fraid you keel me when boy lost in wood. Bob one good dog, he fine heme quick. Bob worth ten thousand dollar!"

Bob went with the family when they moved to Beaver Island. Some new friends of the Whitney family did not understand how important Bob was, and wondered why they kept him.

I remember one day Uncle Loaney coming in and saying to Father, "Mr. Whitney, why don't you kill that old dog? He is good for nothing and can't stand up any more."

Charley and I began to cry and then tears rolled down poor old Grandpa's cheeks. Father quickly explained to

Uncle Loaney what a long time Bob had lived with Grandpa and how he had saved Toney's life. Uncle Loaney was really sorry then and said, "Yes, let poor Bob live as long as he can." After that he and his wife sent many little pails of milk to Bob.

Bob finally did die. We were all sad over the faithful dog's death. It was several weeks before Grandpa and I could feel it was for the best. We buried him where the birds sang first in the spring.